Gerrymandering: America's Coup D'état

René Díaz-Corzo

Copyright © 2023 René Díaz-Corzo

All rights reserved.

ISBN: 9798399155418

I am deeply grateful to all who displayed remarkable patience and tolerance as I withdrew from society.

CONTENTS

	Acknowledgments	i
1	Gerrymandering	1
2	Signs of Autocracy	15
3	Second Amendment	49
4	Authoritarianism	55
5	Education	67
6	Medley of Originality	85

ACKNOWLEDGMENTS

I extend my heartfelt appreciation to the talented and respectful individuals who have gracefully embraced philosophical disagreements and fostered intellectual growth and understanding. Furthermore, I wish to extend my deepest admiration to the visionary architects of our constitution. Their profound thoughts and beliefs, guided by a divine light, have laid the foundation for our society, and shaped the course of our shared destiny. Their wisdom and foresight continue to inspire and resonate, and I humbly acknowledge their profound influence on the narrative of this book.

I am truly indebted to all those who have contributed to this project, both directly and indirectly. Your support, encouragement, and insights have been instrumental in bringing this work to fruition. Thank you for being an integral part of this creative journey.

GERRYMANDERING

The Founding Fathers, through the Constitution, bestowed upon "we the people" a republic and made us responsible for its governance. They recognized that the principles outlined in this document would rely on the actions of its guardians, both good and bad. Concerned about the tyranny of the majority, they set up foundational principles and a system of governance that safeguarded the rights of minorities through constitutional protections. They entrusted future generations with the task of giving tangible meaning to these broad principles, allowing the

Gerrymandering: America's Coup D'état

Constitution to evolve and adapt alongside customs, traditions, principles, and judicial decisions. Democracy, like the Constitution, is a living system of government that can only thrive when free men and women can pursue their desires and aspirations. Even today, these principles are still the most enlightened form of governance in the world, with the United States leading in the implementation and practice of this symbolic form of government. While the United States still functions as a democracy in 2023, the foundations of its democratic system are constantly under attack from political turbulence. One concerning trend is the rising popularity of authoritarianism, the oldest form of government in human history. American democracy cannot afford to disregard the growing momentum of far-reaching groups and the support of base voters for the shifting political culture of the far-right party.

This situation is worrisome, as this party flouts democratic norms and aligns itself more closely with authoritarian systems. Unfortunately, the other leading party has done little, both philosophically and morally, to counter the anti-democratic rhetoric of the far right, which denies the citizenry inherent individual rights and equality. Today, an increasing number of elected officials in our democratic government defiantly reject political pluralism and implement policies driven by unfounded fears of a decaying society. Some argue that democracy involves the threat of tolerating excessive freedoms, allowing everyone to function as they please rather than what is best for the majority. It is important to note that while this argument highlights potential concerns, it does not necessarily capture the full picture of democracy. Democracy is a complex system with various interpretations and implementations around the world. Many proponents of democracy argue that it provides a framework for protecting individual rights, promoting inclusivity, and facilitating decision-making processes that consider the needs and desires of the majority.

The concept of freedom in democracy encompasses various aspects, such as freedom of speech, expression, assembly, and individual liberties. These freedoms are considered fundamental to democratic societies as they allow citizens to voice their opinions, participate in deliberation processes, and hold their governments accountable.

Any trade-off between freedom and the greater good should be approached cautiously. While there may be situations where curtailing certain freedoms appears necessary to address pressing issues or safeguard collective interests, surrendering even a small portion of freedom poses the risk of infringing upon individual rights and creating a precedent for further encroachments. Once freedoms are relinquished, reclaiming them can be an arduous task, as it requires reversing established norms, changing societal perceptions, and challenging the status quo.

However, freedom must prevail as a critical element in democracy, and surrendering any amount of freedom in the name of a greater good will prove exceedingly difficult to regain. Political paradoxes have taken center stage, with the deliberate dissemination of deceptive information designed to undermine our ability to discern truth. These manipulative statements, spread through various media channels, challenge civility, and erode institutional trustworthiness. They are not mere rumors, but strategic tools aimed at achieving set goals through misinformation, pitting citizens against each other. These unscrupulous tactics, carefully crafted to advance the agendas of the majority in power at the expense of the minority, are damaging to the fabric of democracy. The individual vote holds significant value and should be approached with thoughtfulness and investment by every eligible citizen privileged to take part. During elections, individuals and institutions will seek your vote repeatedly. Consider your choices rationally before committing or abstaining, as there will always be a choice that motivates your sense of social responsibility. Not voting carries long-term costs that outweigh any short-term benefits. It is a fact that people develop attitudes towards the political system based on its integrity and transparency, particularly in processes such as elections. Over the years, weaknesses in the American electoral process have become clearer. Ruthless campaign rhetoric has deepened political party divisions and eroded public trust in the electoral process, thereby undermining the legitimacy of American elections. It is alarming that the average voter turnout rate for federal elections from 2002 to 2020 stands at a mere 51.9% of all registered voters in the United States. We are aware that the terms of these groups in the office are up for renewal every two to four years. It is time to change our approach and move forward instead of going in circles. Our individual voting power grants us the right to demand accountability from those in office and hold them responsible for their actions. We must recognize that voter fatigue creates an opportunity for political decay to emerge from internal factors, which arise from the rapid societal progress that surpasses the current agenda of elected officials. Unfortunately, America's political development is currently paralyzed by indecision and a lack of sensitivity to the present realities in society and politics. The government was created by "We the People" to serve us, not the other way around. However, when our rights obstruct the goals of the government or its temporary leaders, we suffer the consequences.

#

It is important to remember that all nine Justices on the Supreme Court were vetted and appointed by the same political system that is manipulative, detached from reality, and sees no practical limits to its power. As a result, the highest court has shown gratitude by becoming a cunning collaborator with those who provided their positions, allowing for a gradual and continuous expansion of government power. The primary purpose of the U.S. government is to safeguard our rights, and any actions that prioritize government goals over our rights are unconstitutional. In the United States, there exists a peculiar irony when it comes to politicians, politics, and government actions. Each region competes theoretically for diverse cultural and socio-economic advantages, all under the guise of a common approach. However, policy gains and retains power without truly representing society in an equal and inclusive manner. This ongoing practice of unbalanced democracy brings out the worst aspects of human nature. Currently, America's demographic boundaries, as defined by the two major political parties, clash with the country's ethnic, social, and cultural composition.

We cannot choose the history we inherit, but we can choose how we respond to it.

When inequities arising from poor governance disrupt social harmony, we must analyze and study these events objectively, finding patterns and addressing the root causes. By doing so, we believe that we can shape an all-inclusive future. A hypothesis becomes a compelling argument when it is supported by reasoning and evidence. This proposition is based on the opinion that, in the United States, citizens increasingly doubt that their votes can influence the government. Further examination of this issue will reveal suppressed similarities and shed light on the manipulation of electoral boundaries, also known as gerrymandering.

#

The practice of gerrymandering has existed in the United States for a long time, with its first public mention in the Boston-Gazette in 1812. Originally called "Gerrymander," it described the manipulation and reshaping of electoral districts to resemble a salamander.

Gerrymandering continues to be employed as a partisan tool, designed to protect, and consolidate political power.

Gerrymandering: America's Coup D'état

Unfortunately, many people are unfamiliar with gerrymandering or simply do not care about it when considering the broader concept of manipulation. However, gerrymandering divides communities, distorts legislative democracy, and obstructs the will of voters, as election outcomes no longer align with their preferences.

While redistricting is intended to ensure fairness in our representative democracy, gerrymandering, on the other hand, is a divisive tool that is sometimes used during the process to redraw electoral boundaries in favor of a single political party's interests. Gerrymandering undermines the electoral process, weakening the impact of votes. This morally questionable and undemocratic practice lacks a clear definition, making it difficult to identify and address. Illegitimately drawn district lines serve the clear purpose of maximizing the seats held by the party in control of the redistricting process.

Gerrymandering: America's Coup D'état

Gerrymandering involves not only randomly shifting boundary lines but also manipulating geographic entity codes and Census Bureau demographic data to strategically populate districts to influence future elections. Parties may "pack" districts with a supermajority of a particular group or "crack" a group among several districts to deny them a majority. As a result, gerrymandering disproportionately affects minority groups, jeopardizing their civil, political, unenumerated, and social rights. Although Republicans have historically benefited more from partisan gerrymandering than Democrats, if this unchecked practice continues, it will only worsen regardless of who is in charge. It is essential for both major parties to accept a reform strategy to combat this corruption. In present times, concerned members of any community can directly see the political crisis unfolding at the local government level. However, unless each citizen takes responsibility for addressing the issues, the urban political environment will continue to promote disorder. The belief that the system is broken is false; it is not broken but rather undermined by those looking to exploit its weaknesses. The political-industry system, present at all levels of elected offices, must align its policies with public interests to ensure the well-being of the population. Unfortunately, the political-industry system competes like any other business, setting and manipulating rules that often favor self-interest rather than the public good. Our political system lacks effective oversight to protect public interests, and much of it goes beyond the scope of the Constitution, eroding our democracy. It is important to recognize that the current political-industry system was designed and implemented by our elected representatives, the very people we voted into office. However, as citizens, we have done little to address these issues beyond complaining and expressing discontent. Recycled politicians stay in office because the checks and balances of healthy election competition have been neutralized. We are not removing poorly performing elected leaders from office, nor are we holding party leaders or legislators accountable for their unfulfilled promises. If there are incentives for elected officials to avoid solving problems, public support will diminish, and corruption will persist. We have the power to vote them out, as we put them there in the first place. As the ancient Chinese philosopher Lao Tzu said, "Every journey begins with a single step." In Washington, the failure to deliver solutions is pervasive, clear each year with the inability to create a sustainable federal budget.

SIGNS OF AUTOCRACY

In 1812, during the 12th United States Congress, the House had a total of 143 members. According to the 1810 U.S. Census, the country's population reached over 7.2 million across the eighteen states that had achieved statehood. The demographic composition of this population showed limited cultural and ethnic diversity.

The recorded statistics showed that 43.8% were white males, 39.7% were white females, and 16.4% were identified as enslaved individuals, encompassing both males and females. It's important to note that Native Americans were not included in the population count, nor were U.S. citizens of Native American descent recognized until 1924, when the Indian Citizen Act granted them citizenship if they were born in the U.S.

During the twelfth congress, each elected member represented approximately 50.3 thousand Americans. It's important to note that the numerical figures presented here are not based on scientific data but rather calculated using basic methods and sourced from archived data. However, it is worth mentioning that out of the total population, 56.1% consisted of white females (39.7%) who were unable to vote, and non-white individuals (16.4%) who were also denied the right to vote. In historical terms, an average of fifty percent of the Voting-Eligible Population took part in midterm elections from 1789 to 2018. This statistic highlights the significant role that midterm elections have played in shaping the democratic process and citizen engagement in the United States over the course of over two centuries. It is worth noting that the fifty percent average is an amalgamation of different turnout rates across different election cycles. Throughout the years, various factors have influenced voter turnout in midterm elections.

Political climate, national issues, and the perceived importance of the races being contested all contribute to shaping voter behavior.

The 15th Amendment of the U.S. Constitution, which was enacted in 1870, marked a significant milestone by granting non-white men and freed slaves the right to vote. However, it is important to note that women had to wait until 1920 for the 19th Amendment to be ratified, finally granting them the right to vote as well. Prior to these amendments, the absence of these rights created a situation where only white men who were eligible to vote

Gerrymandering: America's Coup D'état

could control elections and shape policies, even though they made up a minority of the population.

This discriminatory practice marginalized much of the population while empowering a privileged minority to take part fully in the electoral process and dictate policy outcomes. Astonishingly, each congressional district representative, accountable to approximately 160 thousand citizens, primarily served the interests of the minority group that had elected them into office. This system perpetuated a significant power imbalance, as elected officials were more likely to cater to the demands and preferences of the privileged few rather than the broader population.

Over time, the struggle for suffrage has brought about important reforms to address these disparities, culminating in the passage of the 15th and 19th Amendments. While progress has been made in expanding voting rights, it is crucial to continue working towards a more inclusive and fair democracy that ensures all voices are heard and represented. The historical context highlights the necessity of promoting universal suffrage and striving for a society where every citizen has an equal opportunity to take part in the democratic process and shape the policies that affect their lives.

The preliminary findings from the 1870 decennial census supplied an incomplete picture of the United States population, estimating a total of slightly above 38.5 million people. According to this tally, the racial and ethnic composition of the country stood at 87.7% White, 12.7% Black, and 0.2% Asian and Pacific Islander. Although the Census did not specify the number of women within each group, it is reasonable to assume that females made up at least 50% of the overall population. Additionally, it is likely that only a small percentage, if any, of the male Black population had the opportunity to vote during this time.

The devastating impact of the Civil War, a conflict that exacted an immeasurable human toll, resulted in a significant reduction in the male population. While an exact count of casualties is not available, historical research estimates that between 650,000 to 850,000 individuals lost their lives during the war. This loss of life also had the effect of shrinking the percentage of eligible white male voters, further amplifying their minority status.

It is important to acknowledge that even well into the twentieth century, civil rights were fragmented, and political and social rights were not equally distributed. The separation of civil, political, and social rights constrained the range of citizenship rights and perpetuated the subordinate status of certain social groups.

The consequences of this historical context highlight the struggle for equality and the ongoing efforts to expand and protect the rights of all individuals, regardless of their race, gender, or social status. It serves as a reminder of the progress that has been made and the work that still needs to be done to ensure that every person enjoys the full range of civil, political, and social rights as equal citizens of the United States.

Throughout United States history, opposition to universal male suffrage has often been rooted in the belief that men lacking sufficient property did not have the necessary independence to responsibly exercise their voting rights. It was argued that individuals with limited personal interests vested in the community would not make informed decisions at the polls. Similarly, the resistance to women's suffrage appeared from those who upheld traditional notions of male control, asserting that women's natural abilities were confined to the private sphere of family life.

Although American black men gained the rightful entitlement to vote in 1870 with the passage of the 15th Amendment, the de facto denial of this right persisted throughout the southern states until the Voting Rights Act of 1965. However, even after the Act and later constitutional amendments, efforts to diminish the voting power of these minority groups have managed to endure.

These historical dynamics highlight the ongoing struggle to ensure equal voting rights for all citizens in the United States. The disapproval and barriers faced by various groups in exercising their right to vote underscore the importance of continued vigilance in safeguarding and expanding democratic participation. Efforts to overcome these challenges and build a more inclusive and fair electoral system remain vital in upholding the principles of democracy and ensuring that every voice is heard.

Currently, the estimated population of the United States exceeds 331 million, while the 117th U.S. Congress makes up 435 representatives. With one representative for every 761 thousand citizens, the notion of individual citizenry and representation in Congress becomes less tangible. When the value of an individual vote is calculated to be merely 0.000001% of the entire congressional district, it can serve as a discouraging factor for voter engagement, ultimately contributing to a dysfunctional Washington, D.C.

The clear disconnect between Congress and the pulse of America is reflected in its decaying functionality, where policies and politics often seem to share little in common beyond their first four letters. This belief has given rise to the prevailing notion that the U.S. Congress is an inept branch of government, inadvertently providing fertile ground for potential autocrats. Unfortunately, America's persistence in holding false beliefs has allowed intellectually lazy and politically dangerous representatives to govern, echoing Abigail Adams' cautionary words: "remember, all men would be tyrants if they could."

As the U.S. population becomes more diverse, a crucial question arises: Are we, the people, genuinely represented? The growing diversity and unique perspectives within the population call for an examination of whether the current representation in Congress truly reflects the voices and interests of all citizens.

Addressing these concerns and striving for meaningful representation should remain a priority for the United States. Ensuring that the Congress embodies the ideals of a diverse democracy requires active engagement from citizens and a collective commitment to upholding the principles of equality, inclusivity, and effective governance.

Democracy envisions a system where every citizen can express their preferences for the individuals, they believe would best represent them in government. However, when policies are adopted solely to serve and strengthen political parties, rather than addressing the practical needs of the citizens, it disrupts the essential connection between people's votes and effective political leadership.

Voter apathy has appeared as a manipulative tactic and a convenient tool for the majority to suppress democracy by limiting turnout and influencing election outcomes. Elected leaders and the court system undermining individual "natural rights" only serves to create systemic advantages for themselves, perpetuating a cycle of self-interest. Such actions are inherently detrimental to the evolution of democracy, which cannot flourish without a series of political adjustments in the administration of government.

To ensure the integrity and vitality of democracy, it is imperative to address these issues and implement necessary reforms. This may involve combating voter apathy through civic education and engagement, setting up safeguards against democratic suppression, and promoting a fair and transparent electoral process. Furthermore, a commitment to upholding individual rights and the fair distribution of political power is vital for the sustainable progress of democracy.

By undertaking these political adjustments and safeguarding the democratic principles that underpin our society, we can strive to create a system that truly reflects the will and interests of the people. Democracy's evolution relies on our collective dedication to fostering a more responsive and inclusive governance that serves the needs of all citizens.

Contrary to popular belief, the present circumstances or information do not contradict reality, as no American colony has completely severed ties with its past. This fact is clearly proven by the systematic actions that exhibit emerging authoritarian tendencies within the core governance of these states. Surprisingly, more than twenty percent of the population in the United States show a preference for authority over freedom, endorsing an autocratic form of government. While the movement advocating for autocracy instead of democracy is still a minority, it is concerning that the underlying reasons for this shift remain unclear. One could guess with some confidence that there are two general origins for this movement: either it is genetically predisposed or influenced by external factors.

If this theory of social coordination continues to evolve at the expense of personal freedom and a decline in the rule of law, it will lead to a transition from one regime to another. These preceding actions will prove themselves as a natural process, gradually eroding the system's original essence to the extent that votes will hold less significance.

Any argument suggesting that people are corrupt because society is corrupt lacks substance, as the standards for measuring the abuse of entrusted power vary for everyone in society. Such a generalization might apply to a deviant culture or subculture that appears within society, seeking to justify the normalization of corruption through denial of responsibility or by employing techniques of neutralization, such as condemning the critics. In reality, it is our own human courage that is being tested. It is unrealistic to expect good governance from a fragmented and inept society composed of dissatisfied complainers who continually recycle politicians. To err is human, and to believe in claims of political perfection is catastrophic. The practice of recycling politicians has become deeply entrenched in the political system of the United States, influenced perhaps by nostalgia, historical amnesia, or traditionalism. The simple desire for stability in government is still the primary reason why voters continue to recycle politicians. Are these feelings of uncertainty laying the groundwork and paving the way for a modern American version of political monarchy or an authoritarian form of government?

The traditional symbol standing for the Republican Party is the elephant, which is the largest land animal and has physical strength surpassing that of humans. However, intellectually, elephants are considered inferior. Despite lacking self-awareness and moral judgment, elephants have been known to positively affect individuals, transcending fundamental differences with humans. Nevertheless, the domestication of elephants serves as a clear reflection of the transformation within the Republican Party and the declining political awareness among its constituents. This cultivated variation of the elephant embodies the distinctive characteristics associated with the controversial Republican concept of freedom.

It is time for the evolving Republican Party to consider changing their official mascot from an elephant to an octopus. This visual transition would symbolically reflect their enigmatic political agenda. The octopus, known for its illusionary abilities, cunningly exploits misconceptions and diverts attention by employing its many arms. As the mascot for the transformed Republican Party, it would better be their historically inconsistent yet strategically influential political agenda, susceptible to strategic voting. With the party often entangled in shocking controversies, it requires more than an elephant's trunk to keep them afloat and captivate their audience. An eight-armed mollusk can adeptly fulfill this role, with each arm being a different movement or party platform. This orchestrated marketing strategy aims to influence beliefs, sow doubt, all under the guidance of a central brain.

To borrow a couple of lines from Thomas E. Mann "Today's Republican Party...is an insurgent outlier. It has become ideologically extreme; contemptuous of the inherited social and economic policy regime; scornful of compromise; unpersuaded by conventional understanding of facts, evidence, and science; and dismissive of the legitimacy of its political opposition..." This here and now is where the Founders cautioned that the system they designed was suited to perform efficiently in a moral society.

Gerrymandering: America's Coup D'état

The health and survival of democracy rely on the integrity of the electoral process, as the government's effectiveness in addressing the nation's challenges hinges on the unquestionable legitimacy of election outcomes. During the administration of the forty-fifth president of the United States, significant misinformation narratives gained prominence, raising concerns about their impact on voting behavior. It is challenging to find other instances where an American political party showed such careless indifference towards the nation's well-being, undermining the quality of American elections. Despite the courts overwhelmingly dismissing claims of electoral fraud, the harm inflicted is evident. The false claims have further eroded public trust in the electoral process, exacerbated party polarization, and led experts to rate American elections as the weakest among all western democracies.

Misinformation campaigns aimed at undermining American institutions primarily targeted the reputation of the electoral process, exploiting its vulnerability concerning the privacy of voter's personal information. As these fabrications proliferated, they culminated in the first attempted autocratic coup on January 6, 2021. This assault took place at the U.S. Capitol on the day designated for the counting and official certification of Electoral College votes, which determined the results of the presidential election.

In the realm of elections, it is crucial that we keep our unwavering love for democracy and refuse to succumb to the notion that everything is rigged, leaving us powerless to save it. Elections serve as the frontline defenders of our fundamental rights. Through the power of our votes, we can reject those who undermine the legitimacy of political opponents, demonstrate a weak commitment to democratic principles, or seek to politicize vital institutions like the civil service, military, or National Guard while encouraging or tolerating violence. Once these individuals assume office, it becomes exceedingly challenging to rectify the situation. In times when democracy faces threats, every day becomes pivotal to its survival. Let us not forget that the first amendment of the constitution safeguards our right to free expression, even though it also allows the spread of campaign lies. It is worth quoting Kayode Seyi Tayo, who said, "No number of lies can stand the weight of truth."

#

During the mid-2022 live public hearings held by the U.S. House Select Committee to investigate the January 6th attack on the United States Capitol, a range of insurrectional efforts came to light. These efforts were carried out by private individuals, elected officials, and radical political groups, all aimed at undermining the Constitution's authority and principles. There is evidence linking these individuals and groups to the then President and Presidential administration, showing their collaboration and involvement in violently disrupting the joint session of Congress and trying to overturn the results of the 2020 presidential election.

Even today, Federalism is still a source of political conflict, deeply rooted in the nation's political culture and continuing to shape its beliefs and policies. Envisioned by the framers and established in the Constitution, Federalism involves the division of power between the United States National Government and the United States State governments. This dual sovereignty or federal system is designed to protect individual rights and the fundamental principle that all authority comes from the people. The founders believed that an overly powerful national government would pose a threat to individual liberties, leading them to adopt the federal ideology, allowing multiple levels of independent government to coexist. James Madison, in The Federalist Papers Number 39 on January 16, 1788, defines a republican form of government and warns against a strong national government that would wield "indefinite supremacy over all persons and things."

With a government system intentionally designed to be both centralized and decentralized, this structure fuels ideological battles between the two major political parties. Each party tries to shift responsibility for policymaking, seeking to gain an advantage by blaming the other. This masterful design by the founders creates a deliberate sense of confusion and serves as a form of checks and balances.

Over the course of many years, states have gradually increased their sovereignty and autonomy from

Washington D.C. This has allowed them to supply havens for hard-right groups and tolerate their activities. These safe havens have enabled states to experiment with antidemocratic groups that promote conspiracy theories and undermine democratic values, ultimately generating a shared sense of urgency among their members. Through planned actions, these groups have achieved varying degrees of success in perpetuating social hierarchies and impeding the spread of political equality.

#

Undoubtedly, antidemocratic sentiment is gaining momentum within traditional political parties, and it is no coincidence that women's equality is being undermined at the same time as the rise of authoritarianism. It is true that patriarchal authoritarians are apprehensive about women's political involvement and the movements they lead, as these movements strive for a more inclusive and unrestrained democracy.

Women have endured unparalleled victimization throughout history, fighting against social hierarchies that concentrate power in the hands of a privileged few. Today, reversing the decline of democracy in the United States would be impossible without the full and equal participation of women in every aspect of the decision-making process. Equal participation in the political sphere is not only crucial for democracy but also for achieving justice.

Throughout centuries, women have courageously stood at the forefront, advocating for inclusion, and demanding their rightful representation. The successful outcomes of these campaigns have not only strengthened democracy but also instilled a sense of fear in autocrats, who instinctively recognize the transformative power of women's empowerment. This fear is so profound that it requires no further elaboration, as its implications are self-evident.

#

The decision to overturn Roe and Casey by the majority is driven by one clear motive: deep-seated disdain for these cases, coupled with the newfound voting power to discard them. In doing so, the majority effectively replaces the rule of law with a rule dictated by judges.

It is crucial to consider Article VI of the Constitution, which sets up the Constitution as the supreme law of the land. Furthermore, Article III establishes the federal judiciary, with Section I designating the Supreme Court as the entity vested with judicial power. The Court's primary function is to ascertain the original intent of constitutional language and apply it deductively to contemporary issues.

Unfortunately, despite the passage of centuries, the Supreme Court of the United States, with its justices serving lifelong appointments, has failed to evolve culturally and socially with the changing times. Moreover, many of its members prioritize matters of personal morality over constitutional principles. With a job guaranteed for life, these justices may feel emboldened to pursue personal agendas rather than uphold justice.

So, what is the underlying reason behind the Supreme Court's decision to overturn Roe v. Wade, after nearly five decades of its establishment? In 1973, the Court ruled in favor of Jane Roe, recognizing the right to abortion under the Due Process Clause of the 14th Amendment, which safeguards the right to privacy. However, this latest decision shifts the responsibility of regulating abortion back to the states and their elected officials.

While both the pro-choice and pro-life camps have strong viewpoints, only the pro-choice side genuinely defends women's right to privacy and highlights the Court's hypocrisy. When the abortion issue becomes politicized rather than strictly constitutional, legislative actions can infringe upon women's rights, perpetuating societal segregation and serving as a tool for power-seeking politicians. The ambiguity of the Constitution allows these aspiring autocrats in office to cherry-pick and disregard its "sanctity," manipulating the very rights it is meant to protect.

The morally and prestige bankrupted Supreme Court can no longer hide their actions from casual observers, as their failure to uphold justice gives rise to injustice. Adding more guilt and psychological torment to the already difficult decision of whether to have an abortion is fundamentally unjust. This decision should remain between the woman and her personal beliefs."

Respecting individual autonomy and refraining from controlling others is crucial. It is essential to honor and uphold the fundamental right of individuals to make their own choices and decisions, rather than trying to exert undue influence or control over their actions and behaviors.

The concepts of actions and freedoms are intricately intertwined. Freedoms encompass the inherent rights and privileges that individuals must autonomously navigate their lives and make choices that align with their values and aspirations. Actions, in turn, are the tangible manifestations of these freedoms, being the ways in which individuals exercise their autonomy.

One noteworthy similarity between actions and freedoms lies in their shared foundation of individual autonomy. When individuals are granted the freedom to make their own choices, they can actively engage in actions that reflect their unique perspectives, beliefs, and desires. By respecting their autonomy, we acknowledge and confirm their ability for self-determination and personal agency.

Recognizing the significance of individual autonomy needs a deep respect for diverse perspectives and experiences. Each person has a distinct set of values, aspirations, and circumstances that shape their decision-making process. Embracing this diversity and honoring individual autonomy fosters a society that values personal freedom, creativity, and self-expression.

#

Democracy, often regarded as a social experiment, is a system of government that is supported and guided by the constitution, which is considered a living document. It embodies the collective values, principles, and aspirations of a society, providing a framework for the governance and protection of citizens' rights.

As a social experiment, democracy reflects the belief that power should ultimately reside with the people, who exercise their sovereignty through various mechanisms such as elections, participation in decision-making processes, and the protection of individual freedoms. It aims to create a government that is accountable, representative, and responsive to the needs and aspirations of the populace.

The constitution serves as the foundation of a democratic system, outlining the rights and responsibilities of citizens, the structure and powers of government institutions, and the checks and balances necessary to prevent abuses of power. It is often considered a living document because it is designed to be adaptable and flexible, capable of evolving with the changing needs and values of society over time.

Through its provisions, the constitution safeguards fundamental rights such as freedom of speech, assembly, and religion, as well as equality before the law. It establishes mechanisms for the separation of powers, ensuring an independent judiciary, a legislative branch, and an executive branch that work together to maintain a balance of power and prevent the concentration of authority.

The constitution also outlines the procedures and guidelines for democratic processes, including the conduct of elections, the protection of minority rights, and the ability of citizens to participate in decision-making through avenues such as public debate, activism, and the right to petition the government.

In this way, the constitution acts as a living document that can be interpreted and amended to reflect societal progress and changing norms, while still preserving the core principles and values of democracy. It provides a framework for the ongoing experiment of democracy, allowing for continuous dialogue and adaptation in response to the evolving needs and aspirations of the people it serves.

When democracy is trampled, it signifies a situation where the fundamental principles and functioning of the democratic system are disregarded, weakened, or undermined, often by those in power or external forces. This erosion suggests a violation or compromise of the democratic ideals encompassing freedom, equality, and participation.

The rule of law, which ensures equal treatment and protection for all citizens, can suffer from a weakened state. This may entail the selective application of laws, political interference in the judicial system, or the establishment of alternative justice systems serving the interests of those in power.

In such a scenario, power becomes concentrated in the hands of a few individuals or a single political party, creating an imbalance that potentially fosters authoritarian tendencies. The cornerstone of democracy, elections, can be subverted through various means including gerrymandering, voter suppression, intimidation, or fraudulent practices, all of which compromise the integrity and fairness of the electoral process.

Independent institutions like the judiciary, the media, and civil society organizations play vital roles in upholding democracy. However, within a trampled democracy, these institutions may be weakened or co-

opted, resulting in reduced accountability and transparency.

The consequences of a trampled democracy are profound and extensive. They encompass diminished trust in the government, erosion of public participation, economic instability, social unrest, and a decline in human rights and living standards. Ultimately, the essence of democracy, which lies in the expression of the will of the people through free and fair elections, as well as the protection of individual rights, is compromised in the face of a trampled democracy.

SECOND AMENDMENT

The Second Amendment of the United States Constitution has been a topic of debate and controversy, as its interpretation and implications have evolved over time. In the face of significant concerns about gun violence today, it is crucial to examine the possibility of amending the Second Amendment to address the complexities of modern society.

In essence, the evolution of democracy relies profoundly on constitutional adaptability. It is not a static blueprint, but rather a living, breathing entity that requires our active participation and engagement. Moreover, constitutional adaptability enables us to strike a delicate balance between upholding individual rights and responding to the needs of society. It allows us to navigate the intricate interplay between preserving the foundations of democracy and adapting to the ever-changing landscape. By doing so, we ensure that the Constitution remains a living document, capable of addressing emerging challenges and promoting progress without compromising the core principles on which our democratic society is built.

The Second Amendment, with its ambiguous language, protects the individual right to own, carry, and transport "Arms." Since its ratification in 1791, it has also propelled the National Rifle Association (NRA) and its supporters into a position of influence.

The Republican party, particularly enamored with the Second Amendment, has created an ongoing battle against a fictional enemy to preserve the rights granted by this amendment. This raises concerns about the lack of interest or respect for the other constitutional amendments by some Republican leaders, except perhaps for the Fifth Amendment. The ambiguity of the Second Amendment language and the subliminal interests of some raises the question of whether it could serve as a stronghold for future attempts to subvert democracy.

Amending the Second Amendment does not imply a complete elimination of the right to bear arms but rather an opportunity to reassess and redefine its scope and limitations. A well-crafted amendment can strike a balance between individual rights and public safety, considering advancements in weaponry and the urgent need for effective gun control measures.

One aspect that could be addressed through an amendment is the implementation of more rigorous background checks and regulations on firearm purchase and ownership. These measures would help prevent individuals with a history of violence or mental illness from obtaining firearms, reducing the risk of mass shootings and everyday gun violence. Additionally, the amendment could prove clear guidelines for responsible gun ownership, including mandatory training, secure storage requirements, and reporting lost or stolen firearms.

Furthermore, an amended Second Amendment could empower states and local governments to enact gun laws that align with the specific needs and preferences of their communities. This approach respects the principle of federalism while acknowledging the variations in gun violence rates and cultural attitudes towards firearms between urban and rural areas.

Amending the Second Amendment is not an attack on the rights of law-abiding gun owners; rather, it is a step towards addressing the challenges of the modern era. By updating and refining the language, we can strive for a better balance between individual liberties and public safety, promoting a society where responsible gun ownership coexists with effective measures to prevent gun violence. The process of amending the Second Amendment encourages open dialogue and collaboration, allowing us to navigate the complexities of gun rights in a rapidly changing world.

Some individuals oppose the idea of amending the Second Amendment, arguing that it would infringe upon the rights of law-abiding citizens. Republicans argue that they strongly support the Second Amendment, while claiming that the other side aims to abolish it. However, this argument is indefensible because most Americans believe in the right to bear arms, which can still be regulated without undermining constitutional rights. Ironically, Republicans often advocate for authority and law enforcement, yet they simultaneously push for reduced control over the sale and acquisition of firearms, including unregulated and ghost firearms that can surpass the capabilities of law enforcement agents. It raises questions as to why Republicans oppose enacting sensible laws based on scientific evidence and data, as well as why they resist reallocating funding to the Center for Disease Control (CDC) for studying gun violence. As said in "Moral Man and Immoral Society," political opinions are inevitably influenced by economic interests to some extent.

The act of buying a firearm often carries emotional weight for individuals. However, this emotional impulse can sometimes lead to conflicts of opinions and actions, introducing the possibility of undesirable outcomes associated with such influential purchases. While fear and self-protection are commonly cited as primary motivations for gun ownership, it is important to recognize that cultural context, racial biases, political affiliation, and anger issues can also be linked to individuals' decision to own a gun. This raises the question: Are these factors contributing to the creation of an unstable environment where psychological manipulation and pressure tactics are employed to influence specific individuals into conforming?

Gerrymandering: America's Coup D'état

Historically, the decline in civility within the body of Congress has been a persistent issue that has never truly been addressed. Instead of confronting the reality of the situation and looking to improve it, many have chosen to ignore the truth and allow the problem to continue. This lack of action has resulted in a bottomless abyss of incivility that continues to plague the institution. The consequences of this behavior are far-reaching and can have a detrimental impact on the functioning of government and the ability to effectively serve the people. It is important for those in positions of power to recognize the severity of this issue and take steps to address it. Only by acknowledging the truth and taking responsibility for their actions can meaningful change be achieved. It is time for Congress to confront this problem head-on and work towards creating a more civil and respectful environment for all. This will not only benefit those within the institution but also serve as an example for society as a whole.

AUTHORITARIANISM

In recent years, there has been a concerning rise in authoritarian tendencies within certain sections of the United States. This trend is characterized by the erosion of democratic norms, the concentration of power in the hands of a few, and the weakening of checks and balances that are essential for a thriving democracy. The absence of diverse political perspectives hampers democratic deliberation and leads to a lack of alternative policy choices.

One prominent manifestation of growing authoritarianism is the increased polarization and hyper-partisanship that has permeated American politics. Rather than engaging in constructive dialogue and compromise, political leaders and their supporters have become entrenched in their respective ideologies, often disregarding opposing viewpoints. This has resulted in a breakdown of cooperation, fostering an environment where power is pursued at all costs, even if it means undermining democratic institutions.

Another troubling development is the erosion of trust in the media and independent sources of information. Authoritarian-leaning figures have perpetuated a narrative of "fake news" and alternative facts, looking to discredit critical reporting and manipulate public opinion. Undermining the free press, these actors aim to combine their power and control the narrative, limiting the ability of citizens to access correct and unbiased information.

Furthermore, there has been a growing trend of curtailing civil liberties and targeting marginalized communities. Policies such as voter suppression, restrictive immigration measures, and the erosion of privacy rights have disproportionately affected vulnerable populations. These actions not only undermine the principles of equality and justice but also concentrate power in the hands of those in authority, furthering the trajectory towards authoritarianism.

Considering the potential emergence of a nationwide authoritarian breakthrough, it becomes exceedingly imperative for the United States as a nation and its citizens, particularly those at the forefront of societal responses, to deeply contemplate and envision the myriad of social, cultural, economic, and political transformations that may ensue. As people and others who don't fit into the traditional binary patriarchal model will most probably become targets of authoritarian leadership.

Acknowledging the plausibility of such a scenario, it becomes essential for the United States, as a collective entity, and its citizens, who serve as the first responders in navigating societal challenges, to thoroughly examine and project the various ramifications that could arise across multiple facets of life.

By recognizing the potential for an authoritarian breakthrough on a nationwide scale, it becomes crucial to engage in comprehensive reflection and anticipation of the far-reaching changes that may unfold within the social fabric, cultural landscape, economic dynamics, and political structures of the nation. However, it is imperative to acknowledge and thoroughly examine the historical reality that the United States has seen instances of electoral autocracy. This is especially clear in the lives of many Black Americans living in the Deep South throughout the Jim Crow era.

This era refers to a period of systemic racial segregation and discrimination that prevailed in the United States from the late 19th century to the mid-20th century, particularly in the Southern states. It was named after a fictional character who perpetuated racial stereotypes in minstrel shows.

After the Reconstruction period following the Civil War, Southern states implemented a series of laws and practices aimed at enforcing racial segregation and ensuring white supremacy. These laws, known as Jim Crow laws, mandated the segregation of public facilities, including schools, transportation, housing, and public spaces, such as parks, restaurants, and theaters. They also restricted voting rights through literacy tests, poll taxes, and other discriminatory measures to disenfranchise African Americans.

#

It is crucial to understand that while financial viability is significant, it does not ensure success. External factors and unexpected challenges can significantly impact the performance of a business or, on a larger scale, a country's economy. In fact, sustained economic decline can have detrimental effects on the social identity of historically dominant groups. These losses often result in a greater inclination among individuals to enforce social norm conformity, resorting to more authoritarian values to preserve their social status. American authoritarians show apprehension towards diversity. They tend to hold the belief that the growing presence of racial, religious, and ethnic diversity poses a direct and immediate threat to national security. Moreover, they harbor greater anxieties towards individuals from different racial backgrounds as they want to keep and advance their social dominance.

We know that public opinion can change over time and varies among different groups and demographics, so positive changes in an upward economy may cause people to be less apprehensive towards established social norms. Nonetheless, authoritarians exploit the complexity of political ideologies and opinions to manipulate and control others. They possess a keen understanding that these beliefs and viewpoints cannot be conveniently reduced to simplistic binary positions. Instead of embracing the diversity of ideas as a strength, authoritarians use this knowledge to their advantage, employing tactics that undermine democratic principles.

By recognizing the complexity of political thought, authoritarians exploit the confusion and uncertainty that can arise. They manipulate and distort information, using propaganda and fearmongering to manipulate public sentiment. Through this calculated approach, authoritarians seek to consolidate power and suppress dissent, disregarding the value of open and inclusive political discourse.

Rather than engaging in honest and respectful dialogue, authoritarians exploit the nuanced nature of political ideologies to push their own agenda. They exploit divisions within society, pitting groups against each other and fueling societal tensions for their own gain. This undermines social cohesion and perpetuates a climate of distrust and hostility.

Furthermore, authoritarians often exploit the complexity of political opinions to justify oppressive policies and restrict individual freedoms. They use the pretext of maintaining stability and order to silence dissenting voices, curtail civil liberties, and consolidate their own power. This disregard for the diversity of perspectives and the suppression of individual rights are hallmarks of authoritarian regimes.

In summary, while authoritarians may possess an understanding of the complexity of political ideologies and opinions, they exploit this knowledge for their own gain. They use it as a tool to manipulate and control others, suppress dissent, and undermine the principles of democracy. This negative approach undermines the potential for open and inclusive political discourse and threatens the fundamental rights and freedoms of individuals.

#

The resurgence of patriarchal influence can be seen within the context of the rise of authoritarianism, particularly within certain segments of the extreme right-wing in the United States. These "extremist laboratories" have been enacting legislation with some degree of success, aiming to restrict women's access to legal abortion. As a result, the patriarchal forces that had previously experienced setbacks in certain regions of the world are now gaining momentum again, finding a platform within the unique manifestation of American authoritarianism.

There is a disconcerting connection between patriarchy and authoritarianism, as they both involve power structures and hierarchical systems. However, it is crucial to acknowledge that these terms are not interchangeable and possess distinct characteristics.

Both patriarchy and authoritarianism concentrate power in the hands of a privileged few. In patriarchal systems, men typically hold power, while in authoritarian systems, it is concentrated in the hands of a single ruler or a small group. These systems establish hierarchical structures that reinforce the dominance of those in power.

Gerrymandering: America's Coup D'état

Patriarchy perpetuates male dominance over women, enforcing gender roles, while authoritarianism establishes a top-down structure where power flows from the ruler or ruling party to society.

Both patriarchy and authoritarianism rely on mechanisms of control and suppression to maintain their power structures. Censorship, restrictions on freedoms, social norms, and coercion are employed to enforce compliance and ensure control.

Moreover, both systems curtail individual autonomy and agency. Under patriarchy, women often face restrictions on their choices, opportunities, and personal freedoms. Similarly, authoritarian systems limit individual freedoms, stifling self-expression, and independent decision-making.

It is disconcerting to see these similarities, but it is crucial to recognize that there are significant differences between patriarchy and authoritarianism. Patriarchy primarily centers around gender-based power imbalances, while authoritarianism encompasses a broader concept relating to the concentration of power in any form of governance.

EDUCATION

For decades, the United States has grappled with the numerous shortcomings of its public education system, leaving it in dire need of significant and meaningful improvement. However, despite the recognition of these deficiencies, little has been done to address them effectively. This stagnation is particularly concerning when considering the demographics of those serving in the U.S. Senate and Congress, many of whom were born in the twentieth century and therefore products of the very state education systems that have failed to adequately prepare students.

It is important to recognize that the educational experiences and perspectives of these individuals have been shaped by our nation's fragmented educational philosophies. Consequently, expecting them to possess an unbiased and comprehensive understanding of the U.S. Constitution is, unfortunately, a lofty expectation that is likely to lead to disappointment. These individuals, serving as temporary custodians of innovative ideas, often find themselves hindering progress rather than facilitating it.

In many cases, these politicians are politically astute individuals who possess the ability to outmaneuver and outsmart the general public. Their primary concern becomes navigating the complexities of the political landscape to ensure their own success, rather than prioritizing the necessary reforms needed to improve the education system. Moreover, there are instances where individuals benefit from their family lineage and ancestry, rather than their own intelligence or competence, allowing them to secure positions of power and influence without a genuine understanding of the challenges faced by the education system.

One contributing factor to this ongoing predicament is the lack of an engaged citizenry, which further exacerbates the issues surrounding education. When citizens fail to actively participate in the political process or hold their representatives accountable, it creates a void that allows these politicians to continue perpetuating the status quo without consequence. This disengagement prevents the necessary pressure for change and ultimately hampers progress.

In order to truly address the long-standing problems within the U.S. education system, it is crucial to recognize the systemic issues that impede meaningful reforms. This includes acknowledging the limitations of our current elected officials, who may lack the necessary insights and perspectives needed to enact transformative change. Additionally, fostering an informed and engaged citizenry is essential for holding politicians accountable and demanding the improvements that our education system desperately requires. Without these crucial steps, the cycle of underperformance and missed opportunities will persist, leaving future generations to bear the consequences of our inaction.

Education policy at the federal level is overseen by the Secretary of Education, who leads the Department of Education. This position is a political appointment within the executive branch and directly reports to the President of the United States. While the U.S. Department of Education does not possess direct authority over education in the country, it plays a crucial role as an advisory body, providing recommendations to the president and the federal government on matters related to education. Additionally, the department serves as a federal lobbyist and facilitates communication between Washington, DC, and the states.

At the state level, the State Department of Education Director is appointed by the state governor. These political appointees hold greater influence over the education of students within their respective states compared to the U.S. Department of Education. They have responsibilities such as setting curricula, hiring educators, establishing educational standards for admission, progress, and graduation, and being accountable to the governor.

Regrettably, current evidence indicates that many school districts are failing to address the fundamental problems and consequences of the school climate. As a result, schools continue to rely on outdated and unverified educational methods, worsened by inadequate allocation of resources, resulting in overcrowded classrooms and widening disparities in educational equity. This lack of genuine commitment to improving the education system is evident as the education department persists in using obsolete teacher training methods and teaching approaches that do not align with the increasingly complex skills necessary for students to succeed and compete in the twenty-first century.

Without providing adequate professional development opportunities for teachers to enhance student competencies such as critical thinking, effective communication, and collaboration, there can be no deviation from the current trajectory of educational stagnation. It is imperative to prioritize the adoption of modern teaching approaches, along with comprehensive and ongoing training for educators, to ensure that students acquire the necessary skills and knowledge to thrive in an ever-evolving world. By addressing these challenges and reinvigorating the education system, we can lay the foundation for a brighter and more equitable future for all learners.

Furthermore, it is imperative for states to acknowledge the needs of students from working families who, despite their diligent efforts, face socioeconomic disadvantages. While certain individuals in positions of public office and segments of the general public may argue that educational resources are equitably distributed or that financially insecure families receive adequate support, it is disheartening to observe the lack of focus on teaching effective resource management within schools. This striking absence, often manifested in the absence of relevant courses, renders the situation absurd.

One cannot help but question whether these societal realities are the result of deliberate planning. If so, they represent a systematic implementation of a cunning development plan aimed at maintaining power by perpetuating a poorly educated and subsequently socioeconomically disadvantaged population. The phrase "Stupid is as stupid does" comes to mind, and we can appreciate the foresight and progressive mindset of individuals like James Madison, John Jay, and Alexander Hamilton, who, among others, envisioned and embraced the inevitable progress of humanity when crafting the nation's founding document and principles. Unfortunately, their regressive counterparts from the early twenty-first century lack sound judgment and fail to possess the same visionary mindset.

The current state of society is a reflection of its education system, emphasizing the importance of ensuring equal access to education for every member of society. This commitment to justice has the potential to unite society as a whole and preserve the fundamental principles upon which democracy should be governed: reasonably, by the people and for the people. Irrespective of one's present circumstances, continuous learning is crucial, as acquiring new knowledge instills a sense of accomplishment and competence that nurtures confidence. In an educated society, there should be no room for elected leaders who lack competence and exhibit buffoonery.

One of the most striking aspects of the prevailing disconnect in many communities is the lack of intellectual insight demonstrated by policymakers. These avoidable disparities only serve to widen cultural and social gaps, perpetuating a strain of hostility that contradicts the philosophical foundations of a harmonious society. The competitive nature of the U.S. educational system exemplifies the structural failure of America's political system, thereby highlighting a nation divided. This reality is disheartening, as a flawed educational system perpetuates inequality, while education possesses the potential to transform lives, empowering individuals to become valuable contributors to society through their knowledge.

The human mind has a remarkable ability to assign names and labels for the purpose of identification. However, it has come to a point where the seemingly inexhaustible supply of labels for elected officials has dwindled, leaving us without adequate adjectives to aptly describe their behaviors. Far-right politicians, operating as autocratic laboratories within their respective states, now dictate what teachers can discuss or teach in classrooms. This intrusive interference in educational matters has resulted in an unprecedented wave of teacher resignations.

These dedicated educators are worn down by overwhelming stress, the challenges of teaching, low salaries, a lack of decision-making power, and inadequate support systems. The issue of school security further worsens the problems faced by many American schools, ultimately contributing to a growing shortage of teachers. Considering these circumstances, one cannot help but ponder: How did a school system that was once the envy of the world stumble so far and for such an extended period of time?

The aftermath of the COVID-19 pandemic poses one of the most significant challenges for education unless we allow our political leaders to dismiss its consequences and exploit the situation for authoritarian rhetoric. The reality is that the pandemic has caused widespread disruption in education across the nation, amplifying existing racial and economic disparities and potentially giving rise to a lost generation. The educational landscape has been profoundly affected, with remote learning worsening the divide between students who have access to necessary resources and support and those who do not. The consequences of this disruption could be far-reaching, hindering educational progress and perpetuating inequalities for years to come. It is essential that we address these challenges head-on, ensuring that all students have fair access to quality education and support systems to mitigate the long-term impact of the pandemic on top of existing racial and economic disparities on their educational journeys.

#

In recent years, the efforts of Republican-led state administrations to restrict the content taught in classrooms have intensified, with these initiatives gaining significant momentum since 2021. The primary objective of these measures is to prevent teachers from addressing topics related to diversity and inequality, effectively stifling important discussions within the educational setting. Consequently, the wave of teacher resignations has grown more pronounced, particularly in states where such restrictions are imposed. A nationwide poll conducted by the National Education Association (NEA) shed light on this concerning trend. The survey, conducted from January 14 to 24, 2022, revealed that over half of the teachers surveyed are actively seeking alternative employment opportunities, with "burnout" identified as the top concern among educators.

In addition to the prevalent issue of burnout, teachers face a multitude of challenges that contribute to a stressful work environment. One significant challenge stems from the persistent problem of unfilled job vacancies, which places a burden on educators who must take on additional responsibilities or manage larger class sizes. The issue of inadequate compensation also weighs heavily on teachers, with many struggling to make ends meet despite their crucial role in shaping the future of society. Furthermore, dealing with students' behavioral issues and managing a lack of respect from parents and the wider public further compounds the stress experienced by educators.

It is worth highlighting that one issue that often goes overlooked is the state of ventilation systems in schools. A staggering 83% of teachers agree that improvements are needed in this crucial area. Inadequate ventilation not only affects the comfort and health of both students and teachers but also raises concerns about the spread of infectious diseases, as evidenced by the impact of the COVID-19 pandemic.

In order to address the challenges faced by educators and create a supportive and conducive learning environment, it is imperative that comprehensive measures are taken. This includes addressing the restrictions on classroom content, prioritizing teacher well-being through adequate compensation and support systems, tackling job vacancies, promoting respectful interactions among all stakeholders, and investing in the necessary infrastructure improvements, such as upgrading ventilation systems. By doing so, we can work towards a more equitable and sustainable education system that empowers both educators and students to thrive.

Centuries have passed, and yet political leaders continue to struggle in finding a comprehensive solution to provide the best possible education in our schools. This persistent issue begs the question: Is this a deliberate disservice to the nation, with roots in both Washington and the capitals of all fifty states? Could it be that an uneducated society is deemed easier to manipulate and control?

In the current global landscape, maintaining high educational standards is of paramount importance, and the United States must strive to, at the very least, keep pace with the rest of the world. To achieve this, it is crucial to take a deep dive into the complex politics of federalism and examine the federal government's role in education. Understanding education policies can be challenging, as they may vary from one administration to another. However, the undeniable truth remains that we are failing to adequately educate significant portions of our population, resulting in a growing underclass that is unable to actively participate in a thriving economy and becomes reliant on those who are employed for support.

Moreover, a disheartening trend has emerged where highly privileged families resort to criminal behavior to secure enrollment for their children in elite institutions. This not only perpetuates an unequal playing field but also grants unfair advantages to those with financial means, further exacerbating the existing disparities in educational opportunities.

To overcome these challenges and maintain its global leadership and credibility, the United States must address several key factors. Firstly, the absence of a national curriculum hinders the establishment of consistent educational standards across the country. Secondly, societal values need to prioritize education, acknowledging its pivotal role in shaping the future of individuals and the nation as a whole. Additionally, fair distribution of resources and fostering cohesion among educational systems are essential to create an environment that allows all students to thrive, regardless of their socio-economic backgrounds.

It is imperative that political leaders recognize the urgency of these issues and work collectively to implement meaningful reforms. By prioritizing education, ensuring equitable resource allocation, and promoting a cohesive national approach to learning, the United States can make significant strides towards providing an excellent education for all, ultimately strengthening its society and securing a brighter future for generations to come.

MEDLEY OF ORIGINALITY

Commonly said, the United States is a nation built by immigrants and refugees. This notion suggests that the United States would have one of the most culturally and ethnically diverse populations in the world. However, contrary to this expectation, the United States ranks relatively low on the list of countries with diverse populations, with over fifty-nine percent of the population being white non-Hispanic in 2021.

The concept of the United States as a vibrant tapestry of cultures and ethnicities derives from its rich history as a nation that has consistently drawn in and embraced immigrants from all corners of the globe. Starting from the early European settlers to the subsequent waves of immigrants in the late 19th and early 20th centuries, the United States has experienced a constant flow of diverse populations seeking improved prospects and sanctuary. This diverse heritage has undeniably molded the nation's cultural fabric, customs, and folklore, reflecting influences from Africa, Asia, Europe, Latin America, and beyond. It is this magnificent blend of backgrounds that has contributed to the country's extraordinary cultural richness and continues to be a source of strength and celebration.

However, despite this historical narrative, the demographic reality of the United States tells a slightly different story. The dominant white non-Hispanic population, accounting for most of the population, has been attributed to several factors. First, historical patterns of immigration favored certain regions, such as Europe, which contributed to the growth of the white population. Additionally, immigration policies throughout history have often prioritized certain groups, leading to a more homogenous composition.

Moreover, the concept of diversity encompasses not only ethnicity but also factors such as socioeconomic status, language, and religion. In the United States, disparities in wealth, education, and opportunities have perpetuated socioeconomic divisions, leading to segregated communities and limited interaction between diverse groups. These factors can hinder the full realization of a truly diverse society, even if the immigrant narrative suggests otherwise.

It is important to note that diversity is a multidimensional concept and cannot be solely measured by ethnic or racial composition. Nevertheless, the relatively lower ranking of the United States in terms of ethnic and cultural diversity serves as a reminder that the narrative of the nation as a melting pot should not overshadow the existing demographic realities. As the United States continues to grapple with issues of immigration, inequality, and social cohesion, embracing and celebrating diversity in all its dimensions still is an ongoing challenge and an aspiration for the nation.

"We the people have embraced generation after generation of newcomers, waves of immigrants from almost every corner of the earth seeking personal freedom and a better way of life." This statement highlights the historical legacy of the United States as a nation that has welcomed immigrants throughout its history. Immigrants from various backgrounds have sought refuge and opportunities in America, driven by the desire for personal freedom and a better future.

America's tradition of welcoming immigrants, whether by choice or forced migration, has remained steadfast even during challenging periods of civil unrest and wars. This open-door policy has become a defining characteristic of the nation, shaping its cultural fabric and societal development. Each new wave of immigrants, regardless of the circumstances that brought them to America, has contributed to the rich tapestry of diversity and resilience that is the hallmark of the United States.

The path set forth by preceding first-generation immigrants becomes a trail of human resilience, forming the backbone of the industrial development of the United States. Immigrants have played a pivotal role in driving economic growth, innovation, and progress. Their contributions span various fields, including industry, technology, science, arts, and culture. The collective determination and tenacity of successive generations of immigrants have propelled the nation forward, making it a land of opportunity for those seeking a better life.

For immigrants, history becomes an intangible cultural heritage that shapes their identity and comfort. They carry with them the stories, traditions, and experiences of their ancestors, creating a sense of belonging and continuity. Immigrants often draw strength from their heritage, finding solace and inspiration in the struggles and successes of those who came before them. This historical connection becomes a source of resilience and identity as they navigate their new lives in America.

While the United States cannot choose the history it has inherited, the immigrant experience is deeply intertwined with the nation's story. The contributions and legacies of immigrants have become an integral part of the American identity. As the nation continues to evolve, it is essential to recognize and celebrate the profound impact of immigrants on the fabric of American society, fostering an environment that embraces diversity and supplies opportunities for all.

When inequity resulting from poor governance disrupts social harmony, it is imperative to direct our efforts towards studying and analyzing the causes and consequences of such failures. In today's interconnected world, human interactions occur at various levels, leading one to assume that these interactions would contribute to mutual understanding and progress.

However, contrary to this expectation, these interactions often are still superficial, particularly when communities face complex challenges that hinder societal evolution.

When discussing the issue of individuals entering the United States without proper authorization, it is common for people to immediately think of the southern border with Mexico. However, it is important to consider accurate data provided by immigration and border security agencies. In fiscal year 2021, federal officials encountered 1,662,167 individuals at the border who were unauthorized to be in the US. It's worth noting that in fiscal year 2019, there were 2,490,237 new immigrant arrivals, excluding tourists and unauthorized immigrants. This data challenges any biased rhetoric that may be perpetuated.

There are a few factors that can contribute to the perception of authoritarian political views within some immigrant communities. In the cultural and historical context, all countries have experienced different political and socio-economic contexts throughout their histories, including periods of political instability, economic inequality, and authoritarian regimes. These experiences can shape political views and perceptions of government authority. Some individuals may hold more authoritarian views due to their past experiences or the political climate in their home countries.

Migration experiences is another fact that comes in play, immigrants often face various challenges when migrating to the United States, such as language barriers, discrimination, and limited access to resources. These challenges can lead to a desire for stability and a preference for strong leadership or government intervention to address their concerns and protect their interests. To the migrant, economic conditions in the United States, can influence political views. Economic instability and inequality in some countries may lead individuals to seek policies that prioritize economic security and social welfare programs. This can sometimes be perceived as supporting more authoritarian or interventionist approaches.

As immigrant communities settle in the United States, they undergo changes across generations. Second and third-generation immigrants frequently witness a fusion of cultural values, blending their heritage with the impact of American society. These generational shifts gradually reshape gender roles and political ideology. It is likely that new generations will move away from traditional patriarchal norms, as authoritarianism rooted in patriarchal principles loses its influence as a political philosophy.

It is essential to move away from stereotypes and recognize that the reasons behind immigration efforts are diverse and multifaceted. Factors such as family reunification, employment opportunities, and educational pursuits are significant drivers for those seeking to enter the United States.

Gerrymandering: America's Coup D'état

Tolerance is a vital aspect of any society's evolutionary process. Yet, in contemporary times, tolerance has diminished. As a person guided by a moral compass, I strongly oppose the anachronistic syndrome of cultural homogenization adopted by a vocal minority. This practice tries to disguise speculative multicultural biases and undermines the essence of diversity.

When individuals perceive their biases as valid, they are more likely to justify unfair treatment towards others. It is therefore crucial that we reinforce norms that promote respect for one's own cultural identity as well as that of other groups. If these factual aspects continue to be overlooked without genuine introspection, the behaviors shown by these social groupings write down a society that is regrettably embracing unprecedented levels of foolishness.

To address these issues, we must first acknowledge the existence of inequities resulting from poor governance and confront the challenges they present. It is essential to conduct rigorous analysis and research to show the root causes of these inequities, examining factors such as corruption, lack of transparency, and inadequate policies. By doing so, we can develop comprehensive strategies that aim to rectify these governance failures and foster a more equitable and harmonious society.

Furthermore, education and awareness play a crucial role in challenging biases and promoting inclusivity. By promoting empathy, critical thinking, and cultural appreciation, we can combat the superficiality of interactions and encourage genuine understanding and respect among diverse communities. It is only through concerted efforts, driven by a commitment to justice and fairness, that we can hope to overcome the challenges posed by poor governance and advance towards a society that embraces true harmony and equality. Furthermore, recognizing the need for comprehensive understanding and analysis of social dynamics and governance failures allows us to work towards a future where everyone can enjoy equal opportunities and live in a society that values diversity, respect, and mutual understanding.

PLURALISM IN OUR POLITICAL SYSTEM

The two major political parties in a country, such as the Democratic and Republican parties in the United States, do not necessarily stand for a pluralist system on their own. Pluralism refers to a political system in which multiple diverse groups and interests can participate, compete, and influence the decision-making process. While the existence of multiple parties can contribute to a pluralistic environment, it is not solely decided by the number of parties.

In the case of the United States, the two-party system has been dominant for many years, with the Democratic and Republican parties holding significant influence and control over the political landscape. This dominance can sometimes limit the diversity of political perspectives and reduce opportunities for smaller parties or independent candidates to gain traction and compete on an equal footing.

However, it is important to note that pluralism can still exist within the framework of a two-party system. Pluralism can be fostered through various means, such as protecting freedom of speech, assembly, and association, ensuring a fair electoral process, promoting inclusivity and diversity in political representation, and encouraging the participation of interest groups and civil society organizations. These factors can contribute to a more pluralistic system by allowing for a range of voices and perspectives to be heard and considered in the political process.

It is worth mentioning that the presence of alternative parties, even if they have limited representation or influence, can provide some degree of pluralism within the broader political landscape. Third parties or independent candidates can challenge the dominance of the two major parties, introduce new ideas, and advocate for marginalized or underrepresented interests. However, the extent to which these parties are able to compete and influence policy decisions can vary depending on the specific political context and electoral rules in place.

In summary, while the two major political parties in a country do not inherently constitute a pluralist system, pluralism can still exist within a two-party framework through mechanisms that promote diversity, inclusivity, and the participation of various groups and interests in the political process.

The erosion of plurality within the two major political parties in the United States has had profound implications, leading to a nearly even division of the country into three sectors, regardless of the presence of an independent or non-partisan sector. This situation calls for urgent action to prevent further philosophical division and democratic stagnation caused by the two dominant parties, which may undermine the greater societal good. The emergence of a new all-inclusive third major party is crucial, one that can gain traction by obtaining and exercising political power. The increasing voter preference for a third party is evident not only among political independents but also among all Americans who feel that the Democratic and Republican parties fail to adequately represent their interests. Presently, the longstanding presence of political parties in legislative processes is gradually diminishing social participation, driving the nation away from civil discourse and towards deliberate deceit, conflict, and social unrest.

It is important to recognize that social or civil unrest can be triggered by a diverse range of factors stemming from structural shifts in the social, economic, and political landscape. While inequality can contribute to discontent, it cannot be solely held responsible, as it has not significantly worsened in recent years. Politics, among other factors, can also play a role in fueling unrest. A political system that prioritizes division over unity undermines social order and eventually leads to unrest.

The growing demand for a third-party choice extends beyond political independents and encompasses all Americans who feel unrepresented by the Democratic and Republican parties. The erosion of the center ground has been palpable, as both major parties have gravitated towards extreme positions, with Democrats becoming more liberal and Republicans more conservative. However, it is important to note that while independents seek an alternative, they are not political free agents and cannot single-handedly resolve the partisan divisions in the country.

In addition to the opportunity to select a candidate from a competitive third party outside the current two-party system, it is crucial that the chosen candidate prioritizes the public interest over the interests of a specific political party. To achieve this, the third party must distinguish itself from the current political rhetoric and take a bold stance. Consequently, it is critical for individuals and political parties to engage in reasoned discourse rather than blindly adhering to their ideology. This approach ensures decisions are made in the best interests of the country, fostering a society that promotes inclusivity, informed perspectives, and respect for differing viewpoints.

Implementing open primary elections in all fifty states has the potential to result in national recognition for a third party. Open primaries allow any registered voter, regardless of political affiliation, to participate and select their preferred candidate. While both Democrats and Republicans oppose this practice, the latter is more aggressive in its opposition due to the fear of weaker party control. Nonetheless, open primaries offer numerous benefits, including increased voter turnout and greater diversity among voters, ultimately leading to better outcomes for the electorate and potentially reducing political polarization.

An examination of the national legislative body, which convenes at the Capitol in Washington, D.C., reveals the polarization resulting from years of partisan direct primary elections in the U.S. Congress. Candidates must win primaries to secure a seat, incentivizing them to adopt extreme policy positions to appeal to their party's constituents. This trend has contributed to the declining civility within Congress, an enigma that has persisted throughout its history. Since the first United States Congress on April 1, 1789, when the House of Representatives achieved a quorum and elected its officers, the representation within Congress has been nonrepresentative of the makeup of the population. Despite over two hundred and thirty years passing, the Congress of 2023 continues to be nonrepresentative of the public's interests. It is crucial for Congress to shift its focus from protecting the indoctrination process to safeguarding citizens' rights. Upholding individual liberties and ensuring the fair treatment of all constituents should be prioritized. By emphasizing critical thinking and intellectual diversity over indoctrination, elected officials can foster an open society where citizens are free to form their own opinions and engage in constructive dialogue. Prioritizing citizens' rights will strengthen democracy and create an environment that encourages the free exchange of ideas, promoting an inclusive, informed, and respectful society that values differing perspectives.